To

From

Other books in this series:
HAPPY ANNIVERSARY
To someone special, celebrating your
    LOVELY NEW BABY
To a very special BROTHER
To a very special DAD
To a very special DAUGHTER
To a very special FRIEND
To a very special GRANDDAUGHTER
To a very special GRANDMA
To a very special GRANDPA

To a very special GRANDSON
Wishing you HAPPINESS
To my very special HUSBAND
To a very special MOTHER
To a very special SISTER
To a very special SON
To a very special TEACHER
Wishing you happiness
    FOR YOUR WEDDING
To my very special WIFE

Published in 1992 by Helen Exley Giftbooks in Great Britain.
This revised edition published in 2008.

12 11 10 9 8 7 6 5 4 3 2

ISBN 13: 978-1-84634-265-3

Illustrations and design © Helen Exley 1992, 2008
Important Copyright Notice: Pam Brown, Marion C. Garretty, Judith C. Grant,
Clara Ortega, Jesse O'Neill, Helen Thomson and Helen Exley are all © Helen
Exley 1992, 2008
The moral right of the author has been asserted.
A copy of the CIP data is available from the British Library on request.
All rights reserved. No part of this publication may be reproduced or
transmitted in any form or by any means, electronic or mechanical,
including photocopy, recording or any information storage and retrieval
system without permission in writing from the Publisher.
Printed in China.
'TO A VERY SPECIAL'® IS A REGISTERED TRADE MARK OF HELEN EXLEY GIFTBOOKS

Helen Exley Giftbooks, 16 Chalk Hill, Watford, Herts WD19 4BG, UK
www.helenexleygiftbooks.com

Someone very special...

TO THE
ONE I LOVE

ILLUSTRATIONS BY JULIETTE CLARKE.

EDITED BY HELEN EXLEY.

...We are made for loving:

All the sweets of living are for those that love.

Be joyful, unafraid!

THE RUBAIYAT OF OMAR KHAYYAM
(C.1048-C.1122)

HELEN EXLEY®

Our love is like the misty rain that falls softly –
but floods the river.
AFRICAN PROVERB

Love comforteth like sunshine after rain.
WILLIAM SHAKESPEARE (1564-1616)

Your love is comfort in sadness, quietness in tumu
rest in weariness, hope in despair.
MARION C. GARRETTY (1917-2005)

OUR GENTLE LOVE

The touch of your hand in passing,
so light, so swift, that no one else suspects
its loving reassurance – that touch
sustains me through the hardest day.
MARION C. GARRETTY (1917-2005)

The hours I spend with you I look upon
as a sort of perfumed garden,
a dim twilight, and a fountain singing to it...
you and you *alone*
make me feel that I am alive....
Other men it is said have seen angels,
but I have seen thee and thou art enough.
GEORGE MOORE (1852-1933)

Cherish me with that dignified tenderness
which I have only found in you....
MARY WOLLSTONECRAFT (1759-1797),
TO GILBERT IMLAY

My feet shall run because of you

My feet dance because of you

My heart shall beat because of you

My eyes see because of you

My mind thinks because of you

And I shall love because of you.

ESKIMO LOVE SONG

ALL FOR YOU

Had I the heavens' embroidered cloths,

Enwrought with golden and silver light,

The blue and the dim and the dark cloths

Of night and light and the half-light,

I would spread the cloths under your feet:

But I, being poor, have only my dreams;

I have spread my dreams under your feet;

Tread softly because you tread on my dreams.

WILLIAM BUTLER YEATS (1865-1939)

I kiss your hands and kneel before you...

to assure you that my whole mind,

all the breadth of my spirit, all my heart

xist only to love you. I adore you... so beautiful,

so perfect, so made to be cherished, adored

and loved to death and madness.

PRINCESS CAROLYNE JEANNE ELISABETH
VON SAYNWITTGENSTEIN,
IN A LETTER TO LISZT, CIRCA 1847

Nothing is sweeter than love,
Nothing stronger, nothing higher,
Nothing wider, nothing more pleasant,
Nothing fuller or better
In heaven or earth....

THOMAS Á KEMPIS (1379-1471),
FROM "THE IMITATION OF CHRIST"

GREAT TRIBUTES

You are always new. The last of your kisses
was ever the sweetest; the last smile the
brightest; the last movement the gracefullest.

JOHN KEATS (1795-1821)
TO FANNY BRAWNE

If I could write the beauty of your eyes
And in fresh numbers number all your graces,
The age to come would say, "This poet lies;
ıch heavenly touches ne'er touch'd earthly faces."

WILLIAM SHAKESPEARE (1564-1616)

I could die for you. My creed is love
and you are its only tenet.
You have ravish'd me away by power
I cannot resist....

I cannot breathe without you.

JOHN KEATS (1795-1821)
IN A LETTER TO FANNY BRAWNE

COMFORT AND SUPPORT

Love from one to another can only be
that two solitudes come nearer, recognize
and protect and comfort each other.

HAN SUYIN

Though it rains, I won't get wet:
I'll use your love for an umbrella.

JAPANESE FOLK SONG

In the huge mysteries of time and space
I feel your arm about my shoulder and
am not afraid.

PAM BROWN, b.1928

You are always there for me and so you give
me the courage to stand alone.

MARION C. GARRETTY (1917-2005)

...Love...

the only warmth,

the only peace.

DELMORE SCHWARTZ (1913-1966),
FROM "FOR THE ONE WHO WOULD TAKE
MAN'S LIFE IN HIS HANDS"

The supreme happiness of life is the conviction
of being loved for yourself, or, more correctly,
being loved in spite of yourself.

VICTOR HUGO (1802-1885)

I seem to have only black-and-white memories
before you. But when you came you brought
laughter, red balloons, silly surprises, fizz and JOY
into my life.

JUDITH C. GRANT, b.1960

How sad and bad and mad it was –
But then, how it was sweet!

ROBERT BROWNING (1812-1889)

Love is a wizard.

It intoxicates, it envelops, it isolates.

It creates fragrance in the air,

ardor from coldness,

it beautifies everything around it.

LEOS JANACEK (1854-1928)

Love makes bitter things sweet;

love converts base copper to gold.

By love dregs become clear;

by love pains become healing.

By love the dead are brought to life;

by love a king is made a slave.

JALAL AL-DIN RUMI (1207-1273)

In dreams and in love

there are no

impossibilities.

JANUS ARONY

A DEDICATION TO LOVE

To love is to take the greatest risk of all.
It is to give one's future and one's happiness
into another's hands.
It is to allow oneself to trust without reserve.
It is to accept vulnerability.
And this is how I love you.

HELEN THOMSON, b.1943

Set me as a seal upon thine heart, as a seal
upon thine arm; for love is strong as death;
jealousy is cruel as the grave; the coals
thereof are coals of fire, which hath a most
vehement flame. Many waters cannot quench love,
neither can the floods drown it.

FROM "SOLOMON'S SONG"

I love thee with the breath,
Smiles, tears, of all my life.

ELIZABETH BARRETT BROWNING (1806-1861)

You could give yourself to another, but none
could love you more purely or more completely
than I did. To none could your happiness be holier,
as it was to me, and always will be.
My whole experience, everything that lives
within me, everything, my most precious,
I devote to you, and if I try to ennoble myself,
this is done in order to become ever
worthier of you, to make you even happier.

JOHANN CHRISTOPH FRIEDRICH VON SCHILLER
(1759-1805), TO LOTTE VON LENGEFELD

ALWAYS THERE FOR ME

I love you for the smallest things;
bluebells on my desk, a pat on the head
when I made an awful speech, a cup of tea
in the middle of a deadline panic,
being the only one to tell me that the green skirt
really does make me look like a sack of potatoes
And the big things; giving me all the best things
in your life, sharing my joys, being kind
to me in all my failings and giving me courage.

HELEN THOMSON, b.1943

Whenever I've needed someone to share my joy
or someone to hold me when my world
rips to pieces, you're there. And I know you
will be – tomorrow, always.

MAYA V. PATEL, b.1943

We are busy people, you and I. To accomplish
what we do, we have to stave off all distractions
and give up many special pleasures for the work
we do. But our love is always there. True.
Constant. Sure. Success or failure will hardly
touch me if our venture falls apart at the seams.
You will be there.

JESSE O'NEILL

Those days of freedom can be anywhere.
Long silver beaches. Tangled alleyways.
Temples against the skyline... churches resonant
with song. Merry go rounds. Coral reefs.
A rambling *pension* in Provence.
But always at the heart of them a quiet room,
high ceilinged, bright with sunlight,
a great white bed. And you.

PAM BROWN, b.1928

TOGETHER

To get the full value of joy you must have
someone to divide it with.

MARK TWAIN (1835-1910)

There shall be such a oneness
between you that when one weeps,
the other shall taste salt.

PROVERB

When two people love each other,
they don't look at each other,
they look in the same direction.
GINGER ROGERS (1911-1995)

That is the true season of love, when we
believe that we alone can love, that no one
could ever have loved so before us,
and no one will love in the same way after us.
JOHANN WOLFGANG VON GOETHE (1749-1832)

To lie with you under a ceiling bright
with shifting water shadows –
that's good. To drowse in flower-scented
darkness – that's good.
But best of all is rain – drumming,
roaring, gushing from the guttering –
and we two warm and dry
and safe together, in each other's arms.
PAM BROWN, b.1928

When you have gone away,
No flowers more, methinks, will be –
No maple leaves in all the world –
Till you come back to me.
YANAGIWARA YASU-KO (1783-1866)

All that love loses half its pleasure
if you are not there to share it.
CLARA ORTEGA, b.1955

Please suggest a remedy to stop me trembling
with joy like a lunatic when I receive
and read your letters....
You have given me a gift such as I never
even dreamt of finding in this life.

FRANZ KAFKA (1883-1924)

The heap of blankets on our bed,
the squash shirts hanging on the door,
your tools on the kitchen table, the smell
of your toothpaste. Memories. Good memories.
Touches of you that stay in our home
and keep me close whenever you are gone.

HELEN THOMSON, b.1943

Even nights when I sleep alone
I set the pillows side by side:
One is my love –
Holding it close, I sleep.

JAPANESE FOLK SONG

EVERYTHING TO ME

For love, all love of other sights controls
And makes one little room, an everywhere.

JOHN DONNE (1572-1631)

Your words dispel all the care in the world
and make me happy... They are as
necessary to me now as sunlight and air...
Your words are my food, your breath
my wine – you are everything to me.

SARAH BERNHARDT (1844-1923)

Love is not to be reason'd down, or lost
In high ambition or a thirst of greatness;
'Tis second life, it grows into the soul
Warms every vein, and beats in every pulse.

JOSEPH ADDISON (1672-1719)

It is a short word, but it contains all:
it means the body, the soul, the life,
the entire being. We feel it as we feel
the warmth of the blood, we breathe it
as we breathe the air, we carry it
in ourselves as we carry our thoughts.
Nothing more exists for us.
It is not a word; it is an
inexpressible state indicated by
four letters....
GUY DE MAUPASSANT (1850-1893)

...if we never met again in our lives I should feel
that somehow the whole adventure of existence
was justified by my having met you.
LEWIS MUMFORD (1895-1990),
TO HIS WIFE

YOUR GIFT TO ME

You give me thoughtful gifts –
sugar almonds, a Vivaldi album,
white home-grown chrysanthemums
for my bedside table,
a surprise walk through
the bluebell woods.
But the best thing is when
I surprise you deep at work or
you spot me in a crowd and your eyes
light up with pleasure.
For me, the best thing
is to know how much you love me.

HELEN EXLEY

There is only one happiness in life,
to love and be loved.

GEORGE SAND
(AMANDINE AURORE LUCIE DUPIN,
BARONNE DUDEVANT)

Two things cannot alter,
Since Time was, nor today:
The flowing of water;
And Love's strange, sweet way.
JAPANESE LYRIC

Love, all alike, no season
knows, nor clime
Nor hours, days, months,
which are
the rags of time.
JOHN DONNE (1572-1631)
FROM "THE SUN RISING"

Until you're a hundred,
Until I'm ninety-nine,
Together
Until white hair grows.
JAPANESE FOLK SONG

FOREVER

Doubt thou the stars are fire;

Doubt that the sun doth move;

Doubt truth to be a liar;

But never doubt I love.

WILLIAM SHAKESPEARE (1564-1616)

Time flies, suns rise, and shadows fall –

Let them go by, for love is over all.

FOUND ON A SUNDIAL

Sensual pleasure passes and vanishes

in the twinkling of an eye,

but the friendship between us, the mutual

confidence, the delights of the heart,

the enchantment of the soul,

these things do not perish and can never

be destroyed. I shall love you until I die.

VOLTAIRE (1694-1778)
TO MME. DENIS